Original title:
Tropical Paths to Paradise

Copyright © 2025 Creative Arts Management OÜ
All rights reserved.

Author: Lorenzo Barrett
ISBN HARDBACK: 978-1-80581-688-1
ISBN PAPERBACK: 978-1-80581-215-9
ISBN EBOOK: 978-1-80581-688-1

Garden of the Endless Breeze

In a land where coconuts fall,
And sunburned tourists trip and sprawl,
Parrots squawk a jolly tune,
While iguanas chase the moon.

Flip-flops squeak on sandy ways,
As beach balls bounce in sunny rays,
Ice cream drips on grinning faces,
Each day filled with silly races.

A hammock swings, held by two trees,
As breezes tickle, bringing tease,
Mango slices, sweet and bright,
Turn all worry into light.

Sunset paints the sky like art,
While crabs scurry with quickened heart,
In this garden, laughter thrives,
Where every moment feels alive.

Sunlit Trails Through Emerald Woods

In the forest, squirrels dance,
Wearing acorn hats, they prance.
With every jump, they lose their shoe,
Then blame the sun for the hullabaloo.

Birds chirp tunes with wobbly tones,
As mossy frogs croak on their phones.
The path is bright, yet so absurd,
Who knew trees had such funny word?

Whispering Palms Beneath Sapphire Skies

Beneath the palms, I sip my drink,
A coconut falls, oh, what do you think?
It rolls away, like it has a map,
While monkeys giggle in a funny cap.

Breezy whispers tease my hat,
It flies off quick, just like a cat.
Chasing it down, I trip and fall,
Guess I'm a dancer at the beach ball!

Journeys to the Isles of Bliss

On a boat of dreams, I set my sail,
Seagulls squawk like they're telling a tale.
I drop my hat in the ocean blue,
And now I'm fishing for that too!

Waves crash in a comical cheer,
Mermaids wave back, or so it appears.
With every splash and silly grin,
I wonder if they'll let me in!

The Secret Garden by the Sea

In the garden, flowers giggle loud,
Waving their petals, they're so proud.
I tripped on weeds that tease my shoes,
And ended up in a planty snooze.

Butterflies play peek-a-boo so sweet,
As crabs perform a little street feat.
In this garden where laughter flows,
Who knew nature had such funny prose?

Celestial Sunsets

A parrot sips a cocktail, so bright,
While flamingos dance, quite a sight.
The sun spills juice across the bay,
As crabs play limbo—hip hip hooray!

Clouds in paja-mas start to snore,
While a turtle throws a beach ball galore.
Laughter echoes, waves give chase,
In this sun-kissed, smiling place.

Enchanted Eden

Mangoes wearing tiny hats, oh wow,
As monkeys strut, their own kind of pow.
Vines that giggle as you walk by,
While lizards crack jokes—don't ask why!

Coconuts roll with a silly thud,
As geckos slip, creating a flood.
Fairies sip tea, chatting away,
Giggling about how to brighten the day.

The Allure of Still Waters

Frogs on lily pads do a show,
Singing duets quite out of flow.
With dragonflies wearing blingy wings,
They dance like they're kings—oh, the things!

Ripples are laughing, what a treat,
As fish pop up with a big splash feat.
In still waters, the world drips joy,
Making even the shyest clown a buoy.

Winding Paths of Light

Winding trails are tickling toes,
Where flamingo hats become fashion shows.
Sunbeams sneak through leafy chairs,
While chipmunks juggle pinecone pairs.

Lemonade rivers, a silly stream,
Where gnomes play hopscotch—what a dream!
Each turn brings giggles, smiles abound,
In this joyful place, bliss is found.

Palettes of Paradise in the Evening Glow

In the glow of dusk, the colors collide,
Birds in the sky, doing the glide.
A lizard on a branch, trying to dance,
But slips on a leaf, oh what a chance!

The fruits on the trees wear hats made of sun,
Laughing at coconuts, saying, "You're fun!"
A pineapple wiggles, a mango just sways,
In the evening glow, all nature plays.

Rustic Paths Where Dreams Take Flight

Down rustic trails, a chicken goes cluck,
Frogs hop beside it, wishing for luck.
A goat on a hill yells, "Come join the crew!",
While bees are buzzing, singing, "How do you do?"

Amidst the green fields, a cow strikes a pose,
Wearing a flower crown, with a smile that glows.
Dreams float on the breeze, in silly delight,
As friends find their way in this whimsical night.

Where Time Stands Still by the Water's Edge

By the water's edge, the waves take a snooze,
A crab in a tuxedo, just can't choose.
A fish flips a coin, trying to win,
At the lottery of life, where all fish swim.

The sun takes a seat, as shade starts to play,
While ducks try to figure out a new way.
"Let's start a band!" one says with great zest,
And quacks fill the air, giving all a good jest.

Chasing Sunbeams through Lush Valleys

In lush valleys deep, where sunbeams run free,
A rabbit takes charge, says, "Follow me!"
While squirrels up high keep throwing down nuts,
They giggle and squeal, as laughter erupts.

A parrot on a branch with a hat on its head,
Sings tunes about adventures, making us fed.
Chasing those rays, we spin like a top,
In a world full of fun, we never will stop.

Symphony of the Surf

The waves crash like drums, oh what a show,
Sea gulls dance and squawk, putting on a glow.
Flip-flops fly off as kids take a run,
Who knew the ocean could be so much fun?

Seashells sing secrets, on the shore they lay,
Where crabs do the cha-cha and sandcastles sway.
A beachside buffet of jellyfish surprise,
While sunburned tourists try to fake their cool guys.

The Language of Leaves

The palm trees gossip with rustling sounds,
Telling tall tales of the lost flip-flop found.
Coconuts chuckle as they drop from the height,
As squirrels audition for the comedy night.

Festive flowers wear hats, play dress-up in style,
Bees buzzing with jokes—oh, stay for a while!
With lizards laughing, sunbathing in grace,
They're plotting the next great tropical race.

Island Whispers

Whispers of the sea breeze tickle my ear,
"Why don't you dance? The rum punch is here!"
The sun hangs low, painting shadows that sway,
While tourists get lost on the pickle parade.

Pineapple hats bob on heads like a dream,
Laughter erupts, oh, it's quite the scene.
Even the sand seems to giggle with grace,
As a dog steals a towel and starts to race.

Chasing the Horizon

With a snorkel and mask, I dive in for fun,
Chasing the fish, they're a slippery run.
A turtle glides by with its own playful grin,
While I trip on a seaweed and tumble right in.

The sun sets low, painting skies with delight,
Where the flamingos strut like they own the night.
Belly laughter echoes as we crack our jokes,
On this sandy stage, where the sea never pokes.

Hidden Wonders of the Tropics

In this jungle, where monkeys play,
I lost my hat, it flew away.
A parrot squawked, 'You're such a clown!'
While I searched the ground like a silly hound.

A squirrel stole my tasty snack,
I chased it down the leafy track.
It turned and laughed, perched on a vine,
I must admit, that was divine.

The river sparkled, fish did leap,
I tripped and fell—what a funny heap!
The frogs croaked loud, they joined my cheer,
While hippos winked, not far from here.

With curious eyes, I see a grin,
Nature's laughter, a wild spin.
I dance with vines, I shimmy and sway,
In this wild place, I love to play!

Driftwood Dreams

On sun-kissed shores where coconuts fall,
I thought I'd find my beach ball.
But there it rolled, with such a dash,
And crashed right into a giant splash!

The seagulls laughed, I yelled, 'Hey, rude!'
They eyed my sandwich, such a mood.
As waves came crashing with all their might,
I dodged them while trying to take flight.

A crab waved back with claws so grand,
I offered it snacks, it took a stand.
Chatting with shells, I felt quite wise,
They told me secrets under blue skies.

With driftwood dreams and laughter near,
I frolicked in sand, devoid of fear.
Those beach days glow with silly schemes,
As I ride the waves of drifting dreams!

Starlit Shores of Tranquility

Beneath a sky of twinkling lights,
I danced with shadows, oh what sights!
The fish below thought I was mad,
As I tried to tango with a glad crab.

A hermit crab sported my lost shoe,
I shouted, 'Hey, that won't do!'
It clicked its shell in a sassy way,
I laughed aloud at my beach ballet.

The moon hung low, a gleaming face,
I tripped on sand, then ran a race.
With giggles loud, the night did sing,
'These starlit shores are a funny thing!'

The waves all clapped like ocean fans,
As I tried to waltz with jelly cans.
Each splash and giggle, a tale to unfold,
In this night of laughter, my joy was bold!

The Quiet Call of the Wild

In a forest deep, where creatures roam,
An owl hooted, 'Time to go home!'
But I stumbled on a playful fox,
Who winked at me from behind some rocks.

The trees all whispered their secret lore,
'Watch out for gators when you explore!'
I tripped over roots, which made them laugh,
As I waved politely, feeling daft!

A raccoon with a mischievous grin,
Borrowed my sandwich—it was a win!
I chased him down, but he was too quick,
The forest echoed with my antics, oh so slick!

With laughter bouncing through every mile,
The wild spoke softly, yet full of style.
In this ruckus, I found my vibe,
The quiet call had a jesting tribe!

Secret Garden of Eden

In a garden where bananas grow,
Lizards dance in their flashy show.
A monkey steals my fruity snack,
And giggles as he makes his escape back.

Frogs croak tunes, a croaky band,
While ants march out, forming a grandstand.
In the sun, my worries fade,
As I sip a drink from a coconut braid.

Mango trees whisper secrets divine,
I try to climb, but trip on a vine.
The squirrels chuckle at my plight,
As I land softly, a comical sight.

Among the petals, a breeze amuses,
Bumblebees buzz in their fuzzy fuses.
Here in bliss with flora and cheer,
I laugh at the jungle—my stage right here!

Lush Adventures Await

On a quest for a treasure map,
I trip on roots—it's just a slap!
Slipping on leaves, I tumble down,
Awkward as a wide-eyed clown.

Parrots squawk, looking so bright,
While I confusedly navigate right.
Nature's giggle in every sound,
Giggling snakes slither all around.

To the river, where fishes play,
I throw a line, but they swim away.
The water splashes, tickles my feet,
And I burst out laughing—oh, what a treat!

As the sun dips behind the trees,
I dance with coconuts, feeling the breeze.
Adventures bloom with every mistake,
Here in laughter, I feel wide awake!

A Voyage through Green

A boat made of leaves, what a sight,
Gliding softly, oh, what a flight!
Paddle with a stick—who needs an oar?
As I zigzag past the river's floor.

Fish swim by with a cheeky wink,
My voyage soon turns to a drink.
Splashing and laughing, I spill my cup,
It's a party down here, so bottom's up!

The sky is painted in colors so rare,
Each cloud poses as if to dare.
I challenge them to sprout some rain,
And they giggle back, no need for pain!

With palm fronds waving a funky beat,
I'm the captain of this silly fleet.
In the heart of green, joy's the theme,
Every moment's a delightful dream!

Tranquil Tides

The waves take a stroll on sandy shores,
As I try to collect seashells galore.
But my bucket flips, and oh what a mess,
The shells laugh as I try to impress.

Sunset paints the sky with glee,
Starfish tease me from the sea.
I dip my toes—a splashing spree,
And the ocean's giggle becomes my decree.

Seagulls swoop down, taking my fries,
I chase them away with funny cries.
A picnic turns into a food fight delight,
As I roll on the sand, what a silly sight!

With each wave that crashes with flair,
I find a dance, throwing hands in the air.
Under the stars, I smile and slide,
In this joyous rhythm, I'll ever abide!

Echoes of Laughter in Sunlit Valleys

In the shade of the mango tree,
Laughter spills like juicy glee.
Sipping coconut with a grin,
Who knew chaos could feel this zen?

Flip-flops squeak on golden sands,
Dancing crabs just wave their hands.
Seagulls squawk a comedic tune,
While sunburnt tourists thrash like loons!

Pineapple hats and sunshine shades,
Bikini lines, a laugh parade.
We chase the waves; they chase us back,
Slippery feet in a joyful quack!

Sunsets drape like a neon sign,
As the fireflies start to twine.
In the breezes of whimsy's fling,
Today's mishaps are tomorrow's bling!

Enchanted Journeys through Humid Nights

A wandering mosquito sings a song,
While folks at the BBQ can't get along.
Grilled fish flirting with charcoal smoke,
Someone's hat just became a joke!

Fireworks sizzle, Zippy, Boom!
A dance-off breaks out in the living room.
Sweaty bodies glide and sway,
Tripping on toes in the fray!

Moonlight bulbs light up the fun,
As laughter rises, we run and run.
Crickets chirp their own reviews,
Of our dance moves and bold misviews!

The night whispers secrets we can't keep,
Through twinkling stars in a sky deep.
With each slip, a smile ignites,
In enchanted revelry, our hearts take flight!

Dances with Shadows under the Canopy

In the jungle gym of life, we play,
Swinging from vines in a wild ballet.
Monkeys giggle, they join the spree,
Who needs a map when you have glee?

Sneaky toucans with beakful cheer,
Turn around and draw near.
We trip on roots, get stuck like glue,
Who knew shadows had quite the view?

Pineapple smoothies, spicy delight,
Chasing fireflies into the night.
Laughter echoes on every hill,
As the jungle holds its breath, then spills!

Creatures leap with a graceful flair,
We jiggle and wiggle without a care.
Our shadows dance, but who's behind?
Just a bunch of friends, easy to find!

Island Hues and Ocean Rhythms

A kaleidoscope of colors in the air,
As swimmers flock without a care.
Beach towels tossed like confetti bright,
Sun-kissed mishaps take flight!

Surfboards topple, splashes abound,
While seagulls snicker at the ground.
Flip-flops flying, a sunny ballet,
Who knew fun could lead the way?

Painted skies with a sunset grin,
Sipping punch, let chaos begin!
Belly flops echo through the bay,
Who knew we'd laugh the day away?

Dreams shimmer like fish in the breeze,
Every heart buoyed with liquid ease.
Fragments of joy, oh how they gleam,
In island hues, life's a gleeful dream!

The Dancers of the Shoreline

On sandy stage, the hermit crabs prance,
In their old shells, they twist and they dance.
Seagulls squawk jokes, like stand-up clowns,
While flip-flops flail and fall to the ground.

The sunbathers snore, with hats on their heads,
While nearby, a beach ball rolls under some beds.
Kids chase their shadows, but the shadows run fast,
As laughter erupts, ringing out like a blast.

A coconut falls—it's a fruit that can fling,
Catching a sunbather mid-snooze, what a thing!
As giggles and splashes fill up the air,
These shoreline shenanigans, beyond compare.

So come and join in this crazy parade,
With sandy snacks bright, and sweet lemonade.
The dancers retreat as the sun starts to set,
Leaving behind memories we'll never forget.

Laughter Among the Waves

The waves rolled in with a giggly roar,
Tales of old fish who swam near the shore.
They tell of a whale that wore neon shades,
And mermaids who caffeinate on coconut frays.

A crab in a tux, he's quite dapper, you see,
To a sushi bar, he's off with such glee.
Seashells are laughing, worn smooth by the tide,
As beachgoers joke about perfect beachside.

The sun's like a fry pan, cooking up fun,
As palm trees sway, their work here is done.
A parrot's loud caw causes quite the fuss,
While sand castles melt—oh, what a big crush!

With laughter resounding, the fun never ends,
We dance and we splash, making new friends.
For in every wave, a chuckle awaits,
In this sea of delight, oh, how good it tastes!

Songs of the Sunlit Horizon

Under the sun, a conga line grows,
With lizards in shades and a dog in some clothes.
Bananas in hammocks hang high in the tree,
As sun-kissed coconuts sway cheerily.

Fish throw a party, with bubbles galore,
Despite their odd moves, they get nothing but score.
A parrot sings ballads of seashells and sand,
While sunscreen-wielders make castles so grand.

The waves move like dancers who can't keep a beat,
While beachgoers stumble, tripping on feet.
A crab takes a solo on a slick piece of tile,
As laughter erupts, we can't help but smile.

Oh, sing with the gulls as they soar in the flight,
Join the dance with the sand and the shadows of night.
The horizon bursts forth with giggles and cheer,
In this playful paradise, it's clear we are here.

Shores of Soft Light

On shores that sparkle like glittering dreams,
Laughter erupts in unpredictable streams.
A dog in the surf puts on quite the show,
While the fish swim around in stylish woe.

The ladies with umbrellas, oh what a sight,
Every gust of wind is a comical fright.
A beach ball escapes, like a mad little sprite,
As everyone chases it, giggling with fright.

Sunscreen goes flying, it's splattered with glee,
And someone yells, "Watch out! It's stuck to a tree!"
The dolphin leaps high, a true acrobat,
Wearing a bow tie—imagine that!

As sunset arrives with a peachy embrace,
The silhouettes dance, all with cheeky grace.
In this oasis, the laughter ignites,
We sway through the night under soft shining lights.

The Scent of Sea Breeze

Salt in the air, oh what a tease,
Seagulls squawking, doing as they please.
My sandwich flies, it takes to the sky,
Bob the crab joins in, waving goodbye.

Flip-flops flopping, dance on the sand,
Sunburns and laughter go hand in hand.
Ice cream drips, oh what a sight,
Melting memories, oh what a bite!

Drinks in coconuts, silly and sweet,
Watch out for pineapples right at your feet.
The waves crash in with a playful cheer,
Chasing my troubles, far from here.

As night slides in, the stars come out,
Where's the sunscreen, I hear you shout?
We'll laugh about it, with friends by our side,
On this sandy adventure, oh what a ride!

Lullabies of the Lagoon

Crickets serenade, under a moonbeam,
Frogs in tuxedos, ready to scheme.
Fireflies twinkle, winking at me,
As I paddle past, just a bit too free.

Snakes in the reeds, give me a scare,
"Did you bring snacks?" they seem to declare.
With a splash and a laugh, I drift away,
In this grand serenade, we'll dance and play.

Canoes tip over, oh what a blunder,
Soaking wet laughter, rolling like thunder.
Chasing the moon, we'll paddle and glide,
Under the lullabies, side by side.

The milky way spills, stars ready to play,
Where's my oar? Oh, it swam away!
But with each little giggle, it's easy to find,
This lagoon of laughter is one of a kind!

Cascades of Color

Paintbrush skies and rainbow rays,
Butterflies flit, in a dazzling maze.
Paint me a picture, bright and obscene,
Where every hue shouts, "What does it mean?"

Chasing my thoughts like a small buzzing bee,
Honey-hued laughter, sweet as can be.
Let's dip our toes in this vibrant brew,
Splashing colors of chaos, just us two!

Banana trees dance with flamboyant flair,
Next to mangoes, without a care.
What's that? A parrot wearing a hat?
"Fancy a chat?" Oh, where's he at?

With every stroke, we'll brighten the day,
Splashes of laughter, come out and play.
In this tapestry, life spills over bright,
Embracing the chaos, oh what a sight!

Sunbeams and Secrets

Sunbeams giggle, tickling my toes,
Secrets of sand in the breeze that blows.
"Tell me your tales!" the palm trees sway,
As I wander along this sunny ballet.

Sipping my drink, with a tiny umbrella,
I notice the crabs do their little fella.
Flip and flop, they dance all around,
And I join in, making silly sounds.

Secret treasures hidden by shells,
Pirates beware, oh can you hear the bells?
Every wave whispers tales from the deep,
(Or just requests for a better night's sleep).

As dusk wraps up this whimsical day,
Sunsets and secrets, just a heartbeat away.
With giggles and smiles, we bid adieu,
To this land of laughter, just me and you!

Whispering Palms

The palms are gossiping today,
They say the coconuts have gone astray.
I thought I saw one wearing shades,
Swapping secrets in the glades.

A monkey asked for a napkin, I swear,
He's got a date with a pineapple pair.
The ocean waves chuckled in delight,
As the squirrels danced through the night.

Funky tunes played by a crab with flair,
As seagulls strutted without a care.
They formed a band under the sun,
In this silly world, we're all just fun.

So if you wander where laughs abound,
Listen closely to the silly sound.
Nature's jesters in lush disguise,
Make every trip a grand surprise.

Sunlit Shores

At the beach, the sun's feeling bold,
He's wearing shades of bright marigold.
The sands are hot, like a frying pan,
While crabs try to dance, oh what a plan!

Beachballs bounce and flip like fish,
While sunscreen's made into a squishy dish.
Kids are giggling, building their dreams,
A sandcastle moat with wiggly beams.

A pelican drops in, what a view,
Stealing snacks, as pelicans do!
And there's a dog who thinks he can surf,
Riding the waves, giving joy a turf.

As evening falls, laughter blends the air,
The sun dips low with a fiery flare.
With happy hearts, we'll laugh once more,
On these sandy, sunlit shores.

Dancing in the Breeze

The flowers twist and sway with glee,
They're doing the cha-cha, can't you see?
Butterflies flutter on a funky beat,
As petals pirouette in the summer heat.

A wandering snail said, "Not in a rush!"
"I'll join the dance, but it's more of a hush."
Grasshoppers hop in a synchronized line,
While the daisies claim they're divine.

Mangoes roll like bowling balls,
As laughter erupts from the fruit parades.
And the breeze whispers sweetly this tune,
"Join the dance beneath the warm moon."

So let your heart sway, let laughter reign,
In this jovial dance, we're all insane.
With every twirl, let the joy increase,
Together we're dancing in the breeze.

Colors of a Distant Shore

The sunset splashes colors, oh my,
Pink and orange paint the sky.
Fish leap up in sparkly crowns,
As the evening smiles in orange gowns.

The beach is a canvas, forever anew,
With jellyfish painting waves in blue.
A crab criticizes with little claws,
Saying, "Darling, there're flaws in the jaws!"

Balloons float off in a colorful craze,
As seagulls dive down, stuck in a daze.
Lucky shells giggle, whispering lore,
Of creatures who play on that distant shore.

So when you find colors running wild,
Remember the whimsy, become the child.
In the voice of the waves, let laughter soar,
And paint your spirit with the colors of yore.

Paintbrush Sky at Dusk

The sun dips low, a splash of flair,
Clouds wear hues, a colorful pair.
Birds wear sunglasses, oh what a sight,
Chirping tunes of pure delight.

Ice cream melts down, sticky and sweet,
A dancing crab shuffles on its feet.
Coconuts giggle as they roll,
While flip-flops boast of a sandy stroll.

Palm trees sway with a tip of the hat,
While a monkey plays with a sunset bat.
Laughter echoes as waves shimmy,
While sunbathers swim with a splash and a gimme.

Stars twinkle down like confetti tossed,
As night takes over, not a moment lost.
Dusk is here, wear your best grins,
And let's toast to joy, let the fun begin!

Harmony in Bloom

Flowers dance in a colorful line,
Bees buzz by, sipping sweet wine.
A butterfly twirls with a dainty flair,
While a snail slides by without a care.

The sunflowers nod, they never grow shy,
As daisies giggle, oh me, oh my!
A chatty parrot joins in the fun,
While frogs croak out their best pun.

Raindrops play hopscotch on leafy greens,
While a lizard struts with fancy sheens.
Gardeners laugh with watering cans,
Whistling tunes, making merry plans.

In blooms we find our silly bliss,
Every petal holds a child's wish.
Nature's circus, a joyful room,
Come laugh along with flowers in bloom!

Swaying to the Rhythm

The wind whispers soft, a playful tease,
Palm leaves rustle like giggling bees.
Tropical tunes from a nearby shack,
Feet find the beat, and there's no looking back.

A parrot on stage with a microphone,
Sings off-key, yet steals the tone.
Crabs in tuxedos, strutting their style,
While the locals chuckle all the while.

Sandals slap down, a beat to the hop,
With a twist and a turn, they just can't stop.
Hula hoops whirl like stars in the air,
While laughter echoes, spinning everywhere.

The sun sets low, painting dreams in gold,
As the moon takes the stage, a sight to behold.
Join the dance on this moonlit floor,
For every step leads to laughter galore!

Footprints on Warm Sands

Tiny footprints tracing paths of glee,
Kites fly high like fish in the sea.
Buckets and shovels in a sandy fray,
As laughter bubbles like fresh lemonade all day.

Seagulls squawk, wearing their best hats,
While kids build castles, oh look at that!
A beach ball swells, bouncing with pride,
As sunburned shoulders try to hide.

Flip-flops squeak with every stride,
While the ocean waves can't help but glide.
Tanned toes tickle in warm ocean's rush,
Riding the waves with a joyful hush.

The day wraps up in a cotton candy haze,
With stories shared of endless plays.
In footprints of joy, we all shall stand,
As the sun waves bye to the sandy land!

Horizons of Hope

There once was a crab with a hat,
He danced on the beach with a cat.
They sang a sweet song,
But it all felt so wrong,
As they tripped on a big, wiggly mat.

A parrot named Lou, full of cheer,
Whispered jokes that made everyone leer.
With a squawk and a grin,
He joined in the din,
And the laughter was loud, oh so dear.

In the sun's warm embrace, they all played,
In the shade where the fruit trees betrayed.
With a splash and a giggle,
They'd jump and they'd wiggle,
As the sea breeze around them cascade.

So if you find joy on the shore,
On adventures, you never can bore.
With a crab and a tune,
Life's a wild cartoon,
Where smiles grow and troubles ignore.

A Soothing Soliloquy

A turtle named Ted on a quest,
Wore sunglasses, he thought it was best.
He slipped in some sand,
With a wave of his hand,
And declared, "This beach is a jest!"

The sandcastles stood tall but they fell,
The tide teased them back with a swell.
"Waves are just friends,
Who won't make amends,"
He muttered, "I know it too well!"

Under skies painted blue with delight,
A dolphin danced like a kite.
With flips and with spins,
He declared, "Let's begin!"
As they giggled till deep in the night.

So if life throws a wave your way,
Just grab a surfboard and play.
With laughter and cheer,
Cast away your fear,
And brighten the dullest of days.

The Palette of Paradise

A monkey with brushes so bright,
Painted colors that danced in the light.
With a swirl and a spin,
He grinned with a grin,
As he splashed all the world with delight.

A flamingo stood tall with a flair,
Modeling socks without any care.
But the crocs had a laugh,
And snapped in a half,
As they joked 'bout the latest fashion dare.

Under palm trees that did sway,
A sloth took his time every day.
He'd say with a yawn,
"I'll nap until dawn,"
As his friends would just run off and play.

So join in the colorful chase,
Where silliness brightens the place.
With a joke and a pun,
Life's a whole lot of fun,
In this wild, whimsical space.

Under Coconut Skies

Beneath coconut trees with a sway,
A walrus was sunning all day.
With a wink and a grin,
He jumped in with a spin,
To impress all the fish on display.

A goat with a surfboard so bold,
Rode the waves like legends of old.
But he slipped on a fish,
And gave a loud swish,
As he splashed everyone with a cold.

The beach balls would bounce here and there,
With laughter that filled up the air.
From the kids to the pets,
No one had regrets,
As they played without worries or care.

So if you seek fun on the shore,
Just follow the laughter, explore.
With a goat and some friends,
The joy never ends,
As life gives you moments to adore.

Serenade of the Sun-Kissed Breeze

The sun's a jester, bright and bold,
Tickling our noses, making us roll.
With coconuts dancing in the air,
Sipping on joy without a care.

Laughter bubbles like the sea,
As flip-flops play hide and seek with glee.
Gulls are gossiping, sharing a joke,
While beach bums nap with a sunburnt cloak.

Ice cream drips down the sandy toes,
A sweet reminder of summer's woes.
Seashells telling tales from yore,
While sandcastles challenge the tide's roar.

The breeze whispers secrets, oh so light,
"Did you see that crab? What a silly sight!"
Here, laughter bubbles, life's a breeze,
Under this sun-kissed canopy of trees.

Beneath Banyan Trees of Wonder

Beneath the branches, stories unfold,
Of monkeys who once danced and stole gold.
The bark's a stage, a twisty delight,
While squirrels audition, a comedic sight.

Lemonade spills in an awkward twirl,
As a giggling kid gives the jug a whirl.
Dance of shadows, a game of chase,
Under the canopy's warm embrace.

Whispers of leaves say, "You better duck!"
As a coconut plops with a clumsy luck.
Banyan roots tickling the feet,
While the whole world makes this moment sweet.

The laughter bounces, a joyful sound,
Where imagination and silliness abound.
Beneath these trees, with glee we roam,
Sharing secrets of our make-believe home.

Reflections in the Aquamarine Tides

In waters so blue, fish do ballet,
While crabs wear hats and prance away.
The waves giggle, splashing with cheer,
As dolphins wink, "Come play over here!"

Frogs serenade from their throne of rocks,
Wearing stylish sunglasses for the flocks.
Mermaids are knitting, tails in a twist,
As the sun laughs loud, "Did you get the gist?"

Turtles move slow with a wink and a grin,
Sipping on tea, "When does the fun begin?"
Splashing and crashing, there's no time for frowns,
In this wild world where silliness abounds.

Echoes of joy, a sweet lullaby,
As seagulls tell jokes that make the tide sigh.
Mirrored in waters that sparkle and gleam,
Life's a playful, whimsical dream.

Quietude Amongst Hibiscus Gardens

Hibiscus bloom, with colors so bright,
Whispering secrets in the starry night.
Bees in tuxedos, buzzing with flair,
Claiming each flower, a royal affair.

Bunnies hop past with a twitch of the ear,
Sniffing the petals, spreading good cheer.
A butterfly giggles, dancing in air,
As the garden sings, "We're beyond compare!"

Chasing shadows of a soft, leafy breeze,
Ticklish moments among the trees.
The moon peeks in, trying to sneak,
While fireflies join in a dance so unique.

And here we chill, in laughter we bask,
With nature's humor, no questions to ask.
In the hibiscus, we bathe in delight,
Creating a magic, gentle and bright.

Coastal Serenades

On sandy shores, a crab does dance,
Clumsy moves, it takes its chance.
Seagulls squawk, a noisy spree,
Chasing snacks that fly for free.

Sunscreen slathered on my nose,
I tumble down, yet who still knows?
Laughter echoes, waves do splash,
Caught in seaweed, oh what a crash!

Frisbee flying through the air,
Dodging kids without a care.
A dog leaps high, it steals the show,
Takes the prize, and off they go!

With laughter shared and silly games,
The sunny beach will never change.
So here's to fun, with friends so dear,
Each coastal tale brings endless cheer.

Footfalls on Forgotten Trails

On winding paths where wild things thrived,
I tripped on roots, yet somehow survived.
A parrot snickered from the trees,
As I swatted away the buzzing bees.

My sneakers squished on gooey ground,
Each step a mystery, lost and found.
A monkey grinned, with mischief bright,
He stole my snack, oh what a fright!

With trails uncharted, I gleefully ran,
Through bushes thick, where few else can.
The sun would set with skies ablaze,
While I charted goofy forest phase.

So here I am, in wilderness dream,
Chasing critters, a wild child's scheme.
Among the ferns and laughter's trail,
The secret joys of nature prevail.

In the Heart of the Isle

A coconut fell with a thundering thud,
Cracking my head—oh what a dud!
With wobbly knees, I picked up a shell,
And found treasure that was covered in smell.

In the shade where the palm leaves sway,
I took a nap and dreamed all day.
But ants paraded, a marching line,
They thought my sandwich was truly divine!

Cycling past on a rustic bike,
I bumped a cactus, oh what a hike!
Laughter bubbled like the sea,
While friends yelled, "Try not to flee!"

At sunset time, we gathered round,
The tales we spun, oh what a sound!
In the heart of this isle so dear,
We shared our joy, our laughter, our cheer.

Fragrant Blooms of Bliss

Among the flowers, bees bumble round,
I slipped on petals, fell to the ground.
Smells so sweet, wafting in air,
But watch out! It's a sneaky bear!

With bright blooms swaying without a care,
A flower crown tangled in my hair.
Butterflies dance, in colors so bright,
Yet I tripped on daisies, oh what a sight!

Picnics here bring giggly fights,
As chipmunks try to steal our bites.
We laugh and run, oh what a scene,
Chasing critters through grass so green.

So here's to blooms, as wild as our dreams,
In gardens where laughter is bursting at seams.
Grab a friend, and let's make a mess,
In fragrant fields of playful bliss.

Embracing Dawn in Paradise Lost

With coffee spilled upon my shirt,
I chase the sun to quench my thirst.
A parrot mocks my early rise,
While I forget sunglasses and sighs.

The ocean waves do dance and prance,
As I attempt a morning dance.
The sand gets stuck between my toes,
A battle fought with every pose.

Seagulls laugh at my wild hair,
As I attempt to play it fair.
Like a piñata swinging wide,
My carefree spirit takes a ride.

Yet in this chaos, smiles abound,
For laughter's bliss is readily found.
I'll embrace the dawn with cheer so bright,
Even if I trip and bite my kite.

Footprints in the Flourishing Grove

Stumbling through the jungle vines,
My hat's a base for bee designs.
Footprints leading where I roam,
Trying hard to find my home.

Banana peels and monkey screeches,
I follow trails where mischief beaches.
Falling leaves and subtle pounds,
The forest's giggles and its sounds.

A coconut drops near my head,
I muse, 'Is this where dreams are bred?'
Tree trunks twist with curious glee,
As I dodge ants like they're aiming for me.

Yet every mishap brings delight,
With jungle whispers in the night.
I'll dance like no one's watching at all,
In this whimsical grove, I'll stand tall.

A Symphony of Color and Calm

A flamingo in a tutu struts,
While palm trees giggle, oh what a fuss!
Monkeys bicker in leafy slopes,
Cracking jokes about our hopes.

Painted skies in pastel hues,
As I spill juice all over my shoes.
The breeze carries laughter, light and spry,
Even as I stumble and cry.

A parrot perched with sass divine,
Speaks wisdom wrapped in vine.
"Life's a party, don't you know?"
As confetti blooms in evergreen flow.

Colors swirl in laughter so rich,
Like nature's canvas, a playful pitch.
Creating moments without a charm,
In our chaos, there's fun to disarm.

Endless Horizons in Warm Embrace

In the distance, waves like hugs,
As I navigate through sandy bugs.
My beach ball soars; it's lost at sea,
I wave goodbye, not fancy-free.

With jellyfish and flip-flops flashing,
I tumble 'round—oh, look, I'm crashing!
The horizon stretches out beyond,
Waves of laughter, my special bond.

Sipping on drinks with umbrellas small,
As seagulls plot a sudden brawl.
The sun sets low with fiery grace,
I trip on shells in this warm embrace.

Yet in this moment, joy runs deep,
For laughter dances while others sleep.
With endless horizons beckoning me,
Embracing warmth, forever free.

Beyond the Horizon's Glow

Under the sun where coconuts sway,
Lizards dance in a bright ballet.
Flip-flops lost in a sandy spree,
Sea breezes whisper, "Just sip your tea!"

Parrots squawk with a cheeky cheer,
Crabs do the cha-cha, oh dear, oh dear!
Sipping my drink, I spot a mule,
He winks at me—now that's just cruel!

The piña colada's gone to my head,
I tried to dance, but I tripped instead.
Mermaids giggle from the bubbling tide,
"Come on in!" they yell, "let's take a ride!"

Stars twinkle bright as we laugh and play,
Jellyfish waltz in their jellyfish way.
As the night deepens, we howl at the moon,
Who knew paradise would come with a tune?

The Call of Hidden Isles

A treasure map with X marks the spot,
But I forgot the direction, oh what a plot!
Waves crash wildly, the boat's going fast,
As I yell, "Hold on, let's make this a blast!"

Beneath the palms, I search for gold,
Only to find a piñata—bold!
Swinging wildly, it bursts with flair,
Candy cascades, I forget my care.

Local monkeys throw coconuts too,
What a racket! Who knew they could boo?
Dancing around with a mischievous glee,
They steal my snacks—now that's just not key!

As night falls, we gather 'round the fire,
To roast marshmallows and never tire.
A pirate's tale, a ghost's old grudge,
But I just want s'mores—now that's my fudge!

Embrace the Waves

On a surfboard, I catch the splash,
But land on a seagull—what a crash!
Belly flop champions, we hold the crown,
And giggles abound as I flop upside down.

Waves beckon with their bubbly embrace,
But I'm caught up in a seaweed race.
Laughter erupts with each messy tumble,
Oh what fun when you endlessly stumble!

Flipping on floats, we float in style,
Fins flapping around with a goofy smile.
The sun sets fiery, a cartoonish hue,
Painting us silly in a sunset so blue!

By moonlit shores, we share a toast,
To the weirdest days we love the most.
With laughter as loud as a tropical band,
Let's embrace these waves and frolic on land!

Solstice of the Soul

Sunshine smiles with a cheeky nudge,
I dance like a crab, oh what a fudge!
Beach balls flying, they zoom and zip,
A friendly dolphin joins in for a flip.

With sunglasses glued to my sandy face,
I chase a crab in a silly race.
Flip-flops lost, I walk on toes,
The laughter bursts like the waves that close.

Sunsets colors—a tie-dye delight,
And I get sandwiched between two seashells tight.
Friends gather 'round for the best banter,
With jokes that flop like my dog's bad canter.

The stars poke through like a fabulous quilt,
Our giggles linger, sweetly built.
In this paradise, with joy so whole,
We celebrate life, the solstice of the soul!

A Brush with Serenity

In flip-flops fastened, I took a walk,
With a squirrel who fancied himself a hawk.
He scolded the birds in a voice so loud,
'This is my branch! You must leave this crowd!'

As I tripped on a vine, I stumbled and spun,
Fell flat on my face—oh, wasn't that fun?
The plants giggled softly, the flowers did cheer,
In this calm little world, there's nothing to fear!

The sun peeked through leaves, a spotlight grand,
On a banana peel—the worst of the land!
I laughed as I slipped, doing a cartwheel,
Serenity's humor—a joyful reveal!

So here's to the joy of a clumsy retreat,
Where laughter and nature in harmony meet.
Embrace all the quirks of a wanderer's way,
In this friendly green space, forever I'll play.

Serenity's Song

The waves whisper secrets, a tune in the air,
With coconut hats on, we danced without care.
The seagulls laughed at our goofy moves,
As we jived and swayed in our funky grooves.

Sidestepping a crab, I twisted my heel,
"Oh dear!" I exclaimed, "What a banana peel!"
The crabs raised their claws like they knew the score,
In this comedy of nature, we all want more.

A parrot above squawked, "More_fun for free!"
As he mirrored my laugh, what a sight to see!
We joined in the chorus, a troupe so bright,
Nature's farce in the day, under the moonlight.

So let's sing together, a chorus of fun,
In this silly escapade, there's room for everyone.
With a jig and a twirl, life's absurdity sings,
In this paradise, happiness flings!

Beneath the Banyan Tree

Under the old tree with branches so wide,
I saw a squirrel on a banana ride.
He waved me over, with a cheeky grin,
"Join my circus, come give it a spin!"

We tossed acorns around, the highlight of noon,
Twirled them like juggling balls, oh what a boon!
The shade of the leaves fit our silly routine,
With laughter echoing, we were quite the scene.

A wise old tortoise slipped by with a frown,
"Will you two stop? I'm trying to nap down!"
But still he chuckled, a smile on his face,
While I danced like a fool in this sunshiny place.

The flowers chimed in with a rustle of cheer,
"Who knew fun could bloom, fresh every year?"
Beneath the banyan, so shady and lush,
We found paradise wrapped in a playful hush.

Nature's Gentle Retreat

In the jungle gym of trees, I found my stride,
Waving to toucans, oh what a ride!
They chuckled and swooped, in their colorful flair,
As I clumsily danced without a care.

With grass underneath and a sky overhead,
I joked with a lizard, "Got room in your bed?"
He blinked with a shrug, as if to say:
"Here in my hammock, come swing and play!"

From blooms that were winking, to roots that greet,
The forest was buzzing with a vibrant beat.
Each corner I turned brought snickers and glee,
In this wilderness wonder, I felt so free.

Here's to nature's magic, a wacky delight,
Where laughter is sprinkled from morning to night.
In the gentle embrace of this wild, funny place,
Every stumble and giggle is a gift of grace!

Where the Sun Kisses the Ocean

On sandy shores with flip-flops on,
Where every hour feels like a con.
Sunburned noses, ice cream drips,
We laugh till we fall, as laughter sips.

The seagulls squawk, they steal our fries,
While locals giggle, and sunscreen flies.
Our hats are wide, our worries small,
Dancing in waves, we'll take a fall.

The beach ball bounces, and so do we,
Chasing good times, so wild and free.
A crab in a pail is our new best friend,
In this sunny circus, fun will not end.

When sunset glows like a giant peach,
We toast with coconuts, life's within reach.
With cocktails clinking, let's make a toast,
To where strange adventures we love the most.

Echoes of Paradise

In hammocks swinging, we sway like trees,
With drinks in hand, all worries cease.
The parrots squawk their jokes on repeat,
Amid the laughter, life feels complete.

Footprints in sand lead a silly dance,
We chase the tide, forget the plans.
A sudden splash, someone takes a dive,
Shouting "Help!" but we just arrive.

The rhythm of waves, our giggles accent,
As jellyfish glide, we jump, we repent.
With seashells collected like treasures spun,
Each tells a joke, we laugh till we run.

At night the stars sprinkle tales so bright,
While crickets join in, serenade us right.
In this wacky world where smiles collide,
Echoes of fun flow like a joyful tide.

Mirage of Calm

In a shady nook, we sip on tea,
The coconut's grinning, oh, can't you see?
With every sip, our worries dissolve,
Yet somehow our snack plans always evolve.

The breeze carries whispers of laughter loud,
As a pelican's dive draws quite a crowd.
We sketch in the sand with sticks and shells,
Our giggles ring louder than ocean bells.

The sun-drenched path leads to mischief's delight,
Where sandals go flying in pure sunlight.
A sunhat's blown off, it's a comical chase,
In this mirage where fun knows no grace.

The palm trees sway to our silly tunes,
As we dance with shadows beneath the moons.
In this world of laughter and sunbeam rays,
Every moment's a game that forever stays.

Blissful Escape

Pack your bags, we're off to play,
With sunglasses on, let's hurry, hooray!
Forget the clocks, just time travel on,
To a blissful realm where worries are gone.

Flip flops squeak like a comical duet,
While we race the tide without any regret.
A picnic basket spills like a comedy show,
As the ants decide they want in on the dough.

A splash fight erupts, our laughter rings clear,
While a wayward seagull steals someone's beer.
We chase after seagulls, all weekend long,
In a blissful escape, where we all belong.

As sunset paints all with creative flair,
We gather for stories we all want to share.
With a flick of our toes, we bid this place,
In search of the next laugh, our hearts'll embrace.

Odyssey Through the Fragrant Vines

I took a stroll where the fancy fruits grow,
They laughed at my sandals, on my feet they did blow.
The mangoes were gossiping, juicy and bright,
While the bananas were dancing, oh, what a sight!

In the berry patch, I lost track of time,
Chasing lost strawberries, oh, such a crime!
With each little nibble, I snickered with glee,
Who knew a fruit bowl could tickle like me?

The vines overhead had a rhythm so sweet,
A karaoke night for the critters, oh neat!
The grapes held the mic, belting out tunes,
While the avocados shook like careless baboons!

So here I wander, in this vineyard of dreams,
Kicking up laughter with my fruity schemes.
In a world full of colors, I'm light as a feather,
Join me for giggles, it's the best kind of weather!

Trails of Light in the Emerald Oasis

I bumped my head on a palm, what a start!
It giggled and swayed, oh, it's quite the smart!
The coconuts snickered, rolling away,
While I tried to keep up with the bouncing buffet!

The sun peeked through leaves, a playful glimpse,
While the lizards did tango, with hefty leaps!
I stumbled and chuckled, feeling so grand,
Is this a resort or a cartwheel band?

A parrot exclaimed, 'Hey buddy, what's up?'
He juggled my hat while I sipped from a cup.
The skies were so silly, clouds fluffy and round,
As we danced in the light, joyfully unbound!

I chased a lost flip-flop with comedic flair,
While the sunset painted giggles in the air.
In this whimsy retreat, laughter's the prize,
Come join my adventure under sparkle-filled skies!

Gentle Winks of the Setting Sun

As the sun took a bow, painting skies gold,
I stumbled and twirled, feeling quite bold.
The breeze whispered jokes; each leaf had a grin,
Even the crabs in their shells joined in!

I wobbled in sand like a clumsy old pro,
While the seagulls squawked, 'Hey, down below!'
The surf tickled toes with its foamy embrace,
And a wave teased my fancy, a cheeky slow race!

The horizon burst forth with flavors and cheer,
While I waved to the dolphins, who drew ever near.
With laughter 'round, as the sun took its cue,
I dance toward the twilight, with friends old and new!

As shadows grew longer, we gathered for fun,
In the glow of the night, how the laughter did run!
With stories and giggles, under stars we spun,
In a world of delight, where each day's a pun!

Unveiling Secrets of Misty Shores

I wandered the beach, with sand stuck in my shoe,
The tide rolled in singing, 'Come join us too!'
Seashells were chuckling, telling tall tales,
While the crabs waved their claws like tiny great sails!

In a misty cocoon, the sea breezes swirled,
As I tossed back my head, oh what a world!
The waves took a bow with foamy applause,
While starfish critiqued with their five silly jaws!

I found treasure chests full of giggles and fun,
Where mermaids and dolphins were known to run.
I slipped on a clam, oh the laugh that ensued,
As the oysters laughed loud, 'Get back to your food!'

So here on the shores, where mysteries tease,
I frolic with fantasies, all while I sneeze.
In the realm of the silly, the secrets unfold,
Come share in the whimsy, where joy won't grow old!

Cradled by Coral

In the depths where colors swirl,
Fish dance like they own the world.
A crab in a tux, what a sight to see,
Waving claws, saying, "Join me for tea!"

Starfish lounging on sandy beds,
Dreaming of past conquests and breads.
A sea urchin grumbles, feeling outclassed,
While a jellyfish floats by, feeling quite vast.

Seahorses giggle in silly attire,
Swinging through seaweed, never tire.
They whisper to clams with shells so grand,
"Join our party, it'll be just as planned!"

So dive in the fun, let laughter bubble,
In the coral cradle, life's a rub-a-dub!
When the tides come in, don't be a bore,
Join the underwater dance on the ocean floor!

Mystical Waters

The waves tell tales of mischief and glee,
Where mermaids hide snacks and swim with a spree.
A dolphin declares, "It's a beach party night!"
With surfboards of seaweed, oh what a sight!

Squid in a mime act, so sly and so slick,
Changing their colors, playing a trick.
A turtle with shades says, "Catch my cool vibe!"
While a fish throws confetti, oh what a tribe!

A wave crashes high with a bubbly cheer,
Salty like popcorn, it's crystal-clear beer!
Where crabs build sandcastles, sturdy and proud,
All joined in the laughter, a vibrant crowd.

So dip in the magic of waters so bright,
Where fun fills the air and hearts take flight.
Laugh with the creatures, let worries transpire,
In whimsical waters, let joy never tire!

Gentle Giants of the Shore

Oh, the turtles, they waddle, so regal and grand,
With shells like umbrellas, like they'll take a stand.
"Excuse me!" they say, "Please move from our path,
We're late for a meeting—let's do math!"

The whales sing songs that are oddly out of tune,
Riding the waves under the full moon.
"Why did the fish blush?" one whale starts to quip,
"Because it saw the ocean's bit of a slip!"

In the shallows, the rays glide and flick,
Seeking out sunbeams, they dance and they kick.
"Catch us if you can!" they beckon with glee,
While seagulls just laugh, sipping the sea.

Join the parade of these giants so wise,
With humor afloat and laughter that flies.
For life on the shore is one big jest,
With gentle giants, we are forever blessed!

Rejuvenation by the Sea

Grab your sun hat, let's have some fun,
On the beach where laughter has just begun.
A sandcastle contest, who's got the skill?
With seashells as jewels, let's climb that hill!

Seagulls are squawking the latest gossip,
"Did you see that crab trip on his flip-flop?"
With a flip and a flop, all the critters groan,
Even the starfish decide to postpone!

The waves crash in with a slap and a tickle,
As beach balls bounce, what a quirky pickle!
The sun dips low, igniting a blaze,
While laughter is painted across long summer days.

So lounge in the glow and revel in cheer,
Where every splash brings giggles near.
In the salty embrace, don't take it too serious,
By the sea, every moment is simply hilarious!

Lagoon Dreams and Coral Shores

In waters bright, the fish do dance,
A crab in boots takes a chance.
He sidesteps waves with a twisty grin,
While jellyfish giggle, the fun begins.

Seagulls squawk their silly song,
A pelican tries but gets it wrong.
With mischief brewing, sandcastles crumble,
As kids laugh loud and the seashells tumble.

Sipping coconuts, a happy thirst,
A surfboard's waiting, but first—lunch first!
A splash of lime and a slice of sun,
This lagoon life is just too fun!

So join the party, don't miss the spree,
With tropical vibes and pie in a tree.
Dance with the parrots, eat cake by the bay,
Every day's a holiday, hip-hip-hooray!

Meanderings in the Lush Green

In jungles thick, the monkeys prance,
Wearing hats made of leaves—what a chance!
A toucan with style, so bold and bright,
Cracks jokes with sloths, it's a funny sight.

With shoes of mud, the tourists slog,
"The map says left!" says a sleepy dog.
Yet every wrong turn is a laugh-filled fate,
Finding new paths is our special trait.

Lizards in shades bask under the sun,
As butterflies flutter, full of fun.
"Is that a mango or a brain?" you'll ask,
But it's just your hat—oh, what a task!

So onward we roam, in nature's scheme,
Where laughter echoes and wild things dream.
In the lush green maze, we find our way,
With smiles and giggles, we'll dance and play!

Serene Steps on Golden Sands

With sun-kissed toes, we take our stroll,
Along the shore, where laughter rolls.
A wayward flip-flop flies past my ear,
While kids build towers, spreading cheer.

A surfboard's lost, oh what a plight,
Chasing the waves with all of your might.
As beach chairs tumble and umbrellas fight,
We dance through the chaos—what a delight!

In sandy hugs, we bury our fears,
While seagulls steal fries, those crafty peers.
With sunscreen splattered and giggles galore,
It's a beach day frenzy—who could ask for more?

So grab a towel, let worries fade,
With laughter and sunshine, we've got it made.
Golden sands spark joy in every grain,
Come join the fun—let's do it again!

The Call of Exotic Blossoms

In gardens bright, the flowers sing,
With funky petals—what a crazy thing!
A hummingbird's buzzing, all dressed in style,
"Try my nectar, it's worth your while!"

The orchids giggle, the roses wink,
As garden gnomes dance, they don't even think.
With bees making honey in hats too big,
Nature's a circus, come join the gig!

A pineapple wears a polka-dot bow,
While bananas gossip about the show.
"Did you hear what the palm tree said?"
"Let's leaf this place, I want to spread!"

So with every bloom, laughter bursts free,
Join in the fun, under this tree.
As petals tumble in colorful spree,
We're led by the call of nature's glee!

Paints of the Daybreak

The sun sneezed bright from behind a cloud,
Flaring like a clown, oh so loud!
Pineapples wearing hats, quite the sight,
Lemons rolling in, it's pure delight.

The parrot squawked, 'Join the dance!',
As coconuts wobbled in a merry prance.
Flip-flops flapped like fish out of water,
As laughter soared, getting louder and hotter.

Sand castles guarded by feisty crabs,
Each wave crashing down, their tiny jabs.
Seagulls laughing in their airy spins,
A morning chorus where chaos begins.

With colors blending, sky meets the ground,
In this quirky paradise, joy is unbound!
Sipping sugary drinks, oh what a treat,
Life's a beach, on sandy retreat!

Blissful Horizons

Horizons stretch with silly views,
Where flip-flops dance and laughter brews.
Palm trees wave like they know the beat,
Here every moment's a joyful feat.

Surfboards giggle on waves that surge,
Even the seashells seem to urge.
Fish don sunglasses, a spectacle rare,
As we paddle along with flair to spare.

Kites flying high, making friends with sun,
While ice cream drips, oh what fun!
The wind whispers secrets through the leaves,
In this land, even the lost socks believe.

A hammock sways, inviting a nap,
While beach balls collide with a joyful clap.
In this kooky escape, smiles never cease,
Every detail screams of bliss and peace!

A Marina of Memories

Boats bobbing cheerfully in a silly parade,
Like rubber ducks playing charades.
The fish all gossip, sharing their tales,
While the clouds trade jokes over azure trails.

Sandy footprints lead to a comical quest,
For food so good, it must be blessed!
Crabs crack jokes, oh they're quite the clowns,
While seagulls plot to steal your crowns!

Tsunami of laughter flows through the dock,
As friendly dolphins spin and rock.
Sunburned sunbathers dance in a group,
While sunscreen fights the ultimate scoop.

With treasures unearthed in this playful mirth,
Each wave brings giggles, a true rebirth.
In this marina, where memories play,
The fun rolls on, come what may!

In the Embrace of Sun and Sea

Sunshine tugs as it makes its show,
Gold and silver, putting on a glow.
The ocean chuckles, tickling my toes,
As laughter flows like the breeze that blows.

Dancing shadows cast silly spells,
While conch shells tell the best of tales.
With cocktails that wobble, hats on heads,
Jokes jive around the sandy beds.

The waves compose a raucous tune,
Seashells clapping to the funky croon.
Sunsets paint mischief on the shore,
In this giddy paradise, who could want more?

And when the stars come out to play,
The moon serves up laughter on a silver tray.
Wrapped in giggles, we dance with glee,
In the embrace of sun and sea!

www.ingramcontent.com/pod-product-compliance
Lightning Source LLC
Chambersburg PA
CBHW072117070526
44585CB00016B/1480